Allie's Adventure on the Wonder

Erika Adams

Printed by BookBaby, Pennsauken, NJ

First edition e-book printed 2014
ISBN: 9781483533711

First edition paperback printed 2014
ISBN: 978-1-63192-386-9

Contents

Dedications

To Mr. Lewis Carroll himself, for his beautiful and brilliantly strange inspiration.

To my family (especially you, Mom), for all the love and encouragement and for never giving up on me even though I wanted to countless times.

To Dr. Teri James Bellis, whose book *When the Brain Can't Hear: Unraveling the Mystery of Auditory Processing Disorder* gave me so much more than just information.

To Professor Carol Bock, for thinking of me when she found and offered the book to me.

To Professor Carolyn Sigler, whose college course in Childhood in Literature and Culture provided the opportunity for me to write this story.

To all the wonderful teachers and advisors I've had over the years, for their guidance, accommodations, and *especially* their patience. (You all know who you are).

To all my friends, who have always accepted and loved me in spite of the disorder.

JV

And most of all, to all those who continue to suffer from APD or other conditions that are difficult—if not impossible—to diagnose and treat:

You are not alone.

𝒱ᵒ

I'm swimming in a sea made up of the tears of a giant, who has disappeared somewhere. But as disgusted as I feel about being soaked in salt water (especially in such a frilly dress), I feel even more disgusted at the giant. Why was it crying? It was a giant, for Pete's sake!

After struggling in the water for who knows how long, I wash up on shore. Getting up, I see a white rabbit, handsome in his tuxedo, in front of me demanding why I was not at the castle the day before.

That's right! *I think.* The queen is waiting for me!

I run, following the rabbit to the castle. I dry off, but I don't feel as if I'm really getting anywhere. Even worse, the rabbit soon leaves me behind. As I try to catch up, I'm ambushed by animals in clothes, talking flowers, creatures that can't possibly exist. They all want me to stop and play with them.

They scare me, yet I do want to play with them—I'd much rather play than keep going. But I know that terrible things will happen if I don't keep going.

The creatures reach out and grab me, claw at me, crying and screaming that I stay. I wish I could, I tell them, but I can't. They accuse me of abandoning them, being lazy, no fun, stuck-up, anything they can think of. I beg them to let me go, but they pounce on me, smother me, whatever they can to keep me from escaping.

Suddenly, I feel myself flare up like a candle flame—

My eyes snap open. I sit up in bed, taking deep breaths as I adjust myself to wakefulness. The images of my dream still float like fireflies inside my brain.

I have to get this down.

I whip back my sheets, leap out of bed and turn on my light, feeling a bit light-headed from the brightness and movement. I fumble around for my pencil and notebook. When I find them and get back into bed, I rest the point of the pencil on the paper.

Okay. Come on, let it out.

My hand refuses to move. I know it's because I'm grappling for a good way to write this, but I can't settle on the first words. I realize with agitation that the dream images are fading while I waste time wondering how to describe them.

So, I'm running . . . What was I doing before? Was I even doing something before? Where was I going? There was a dormouse in a teapot, wasn't there? Or something? Oh, no. Oh, no, come on, please don't go.

In the end, all I can conjure up are three words: *sea*, *castle*, and *rabbit*.

"Allie! Time to get up!" my mom calls from downstairs.

I look at my clock: 7:05 AM. The knowledge that I don't even have a chance to doze and drown my sorrow at losing the dream, let alone go back to sleep and try to recapture it, turns my light-headedness into a full-fledged headache.

Damn. That was such a cool dream, too.

~~~~~~~~~~~~~~~

Trying so hard to focus on what's left of my dream, it isn't until I get to school that I find that I've forgotten my purse. *Oh, well*, I try to console myself. *Maybe I can go without it today as long as I don't need my cellphone or my chapstick.*

Though this reasoning makes me feel a little better, sitting at my desk reminds me of the torture that's to occur: today we have book reports to proofread. Mine isn't done, and Mrs. Heartred is *not* a patient teacher.

"All right, everyone," she addresses the class. "As I have previously mentioned, you will spend today's class period proofreading each other's reports so that you can polish them up for next week. I trust you have all put your greatest efforts into this—*correct*?" I cringe in my seat as she emphasizes this last word by glaring at me.

She already knows . . . I am so screwed.

"Trade with the person next to you and begin. And unless it is with me, *no talking*."

I hand my paper over to Queenie Decker, who smirks at me with unnaturally white teeth as she gives me hers. I spend the first ten minutes just staring down at the paper on my desk before I begin reading—or at least look like I'm reading. To my horror, I feel tears welling up in my eyes. I try to be as still and silent as possible as I grasp at the meaning of my partner's report, but my mind begins to wander and argue with itself.

So this is about The Hobbit. *Okay, I got that much. Let's see . . . So Bilbo goes on a quest . . . or is it Gandalf? Who's Gandalf? The hobbit? No, wait, he's the dragon, or is Bilbo the ring? Aw, damn it! Why the hell can't I get this!*

Come on, what's wrong with you? You make it look like the world's about to end.

But this is an important paper!

Not so much that you have to cry about it!

Couldn't she have at least allowed us to add pictures to our reports so we know what everyone is talking about? If nothing else it would be a lot less boring. Aaarrgh!

Oh, man, don't tell me you're about to hyperventilate!

I feel so tight . . . I wish I could just shrink out of here . . . is anyone looking at me?

They will if you don't calm down! Or do you want to just drown everyone and all the papers with your tears?

Sure, why not? I might as well be a freaking giant the way I'm attracting attention! Wait a minute, didn't I dream . . .

Don't change the subject!

Fine, whatever! Why don't I just stand up and bust out of the classroom as well? Then I can both crush and drown them! At least then I wouldn't have to look at this damn homework!

Okay, that's not only cruel, but stupid. Shut up!

You shut up! You have a paper to look at!

So do you!

"Is there a problem, Allie?"

My "conversation" is interrupted by Mrs. Heartred, whose stern face peers down at me. I hastily rub my eyes, but it's too late. Without meaning to, I sniff and whimper, making several heads pop up.

"Outside. *Now.*"

I follow her out, feeling like I'm about to be executed. I'm still crying as she shuts the door and faces me. "Now then, Allie, would you care to explain to me why you are disrupting my class with your sniveling?"

As usual, my thoughts jumble around in my mind like lottery balls, not one being able to stay still long enough to make their way to my mouth. What makes it worse is that Mrs. Heartred's face is like a statue, cold and unmoving. As I babble on about how I tried my best the night before to finish my paper but kept getting stuck, trying to get her stone face to show some kind of emotion, she sighs in irritation.

"All right, get a hold of yourself, and for heaven's sake, stop that hideous crying!" Her voice is so harsh that, try as I might, I can't stop my tears. "Oh, honestly! This is unacceptable, coming from a grown girl like you. You are fourteen years old, Allie, this is *not* pre-school—" The bell rings before Mrs. Heartred can finish. I try to hide my delight as she scowls at me. "I suppose Queenie will have to arrange to have her paper read by another classmate now." My delight collapses. *Everything is your fault*, Mrs. Heartred's eyes seem to say as they follow me back into the classroom, scrutinizing me as I pack my school supplies as fast as I can.

I am just about ready to leave when I notice all three Decker sisters—Queenie, Jackie, and Asa—huddled by the door: my refuge. I'll have to pass their creepy grinning faces in order to get out. Frantic now, but knowing it will be worse if I drag it out, I zip up my backpack and pull on my jacket. In the near silence of the room, the sudden *RIP* of my sleeve tearing is deafening. After a brief mortified pause, I yank off the jacket, haul the backpack on and race to the door only to nearly ram into Queenie's arm which bars my way.

Queenie observes my jacket and then my face. "Looks like Little isn't so little anymore, is she, girls?" The two heads shaking in sync, along with the combination of the red, white, and black of all three skirts, are hypnotizing. "Maybe that's why she can cry so much."

My brain is so fuzzy that I barely register Jackie's words: ". . . going?"

"Huh?" I say stupidly.

"I said, where are you going, freak?" she sneers.

"Nowhere," I answer, praying this will get them away from me.

Asa's cat-like smile widens as she says, "Good! Then it doesn't matter whether you leave or not."

"I have an appointment!" I say in desperation.

"Oh, of course," Queenie says in a chatty tone, "with the school shrink, right?"

"Maybe she thinks Old Dutch can 'shrink' her back into that jacket, too," Jackie adds.

Asa snickers. "God knows it works wonders on her brain!"

Their laughter follows me long after I shove my way out of the classroom. My heart and I don't stop racing until I make it to the game-and-picture-filled office of Mrs. Dutch, my Special Ed. advisor.

"Come in, come in, Allie!" she calls me cordially from her desk. "How are you today?"

"Fair," I say—*Great, now I stop crying*—as I take my seat in front of her. Considering how my day has gone already— and the way Mrs. Dutch's gums bulge out of her tooth-filled smile which, rather than cheering me up, only serves as a painful reminder of my run-in with the Deckers—I'm in even less of a mood than usual to talk. I just want to get this session over with and go home.

"Another hard day?" Mrs. Dutch asks in a softer voice. I nod, peeved that I'm so freaking visible to everyone today. She leans across her desk and pats my hand. Her bony fingers poke my skin and her bright, perky face is close enough to make me feel uncomfortable, but she is nice to me and she means well, so I don't want to be rude. She declares self-righteously, "Some people really should learn to mind their own business—even if it does slow things down in life."

My ears perk up. "What?"

"Just kidding," she laughs. "The point, though," she goes on, "is that people shouldn't hamper those who have to work so hard just to keep up. And as for you, Allie, sometimes it helps not to think so much about these things . . ."

Then why do I even come to school at all?

". . . Allie?"

"Hmm?"

"You are thinking too much again, dear."

I hang my head and groan, "Why does it take me so long to find answers to anything?"

She tries to reassure me. "Look at it this way: one day, you'll have an answer that no one ever thought of or attempted to find before, and all because Auditory Processing Disorder, troublesome though it is, has taught you the value of time and hard work."

As if I can afford the time along with the hard work.

"What if a question has no answer?" I ask her.

"There is an answer to every question," Mrs. Dutch insists. "Everything

9

happens for a reason, you know. Some answers just take more of an effort to find. You know what they say: To grovel hopefully is a better thing than to survive."

This makes my head jerk. "What did you say?"

"I said, to travel hopefully is a better thing than to arrive." I don't know how to respond other than with a lame "Oh." "Now then, let's get started on today's lesson, shall we?"

She then gives me some logic exercises to work on. I frown at one:

Arrange the words given below in a meaningful sequence.

1. Police   2. Punishment   3. Crime
4. Judge   5. Judgment

I ponder the question. *Sentence . . . sentence . . .* At last, I come up with: "Someone committed a crime and was captured by the police. He went before a judge, received judgment, and his punishment was carried out."

Mrs. Dutch is silent; this makes me nervous. "Sorry, I know that sounds really dumb," I try to tell her, "but I was just supposed to use the words, right?"

"Yes," she says carefully, "and no."

She passes her notebook over to me so I can see the answer:

The correct order is:

Crime Police Judge Judgment Punishment

3   1   4   5   2

I put a hand to my face, exasperated. "I mistook "sequence" for "sentence,"" I say flatly.

"Well, never mind, Allie," Mrs. Dutch says. Her encouragement feels dismissive to me. "You *did* technically get the order correct."

Excuse me?

"But I wasn't supposed to put it in a sentence!" I protest.

"It doesn't matter . . ."—*What do you mean, 'It doesn't matter'?!*—". . . a good answer. That's what's important. It's not as though you put 'punishment' before 'judgment', right?"

I sigh, giving up.

"Hey, you're being so pessimistic now. Everything will be fine, you'll see."

I pause, but so briefly she doesn't notice.

How dare you.

My time with her is up, so she confirms my next session. As I leave, Mrs. Dutch gives me another warm smile, saying, "Don't worry, Allie, I have complete confidence in you. And remember: Whatever does kill you makes you sunder."

It feels impolite, but I walk out silently anyway, too heartsick to ask what she really said.

~~~~~~~~~~

Thankfully, I manage to skim through the rest of the day's classes. I run all the way home, anxious to climb into bed and seek comfort in my own company (such as it is). I make my way up my front steps and reach for my key . . . inside . . . my . . .

I lift my face toward the sky with closed eyes and clenched teeth. My key is in my purse, which is inside my house, which I can't get into without my key. I want to kick myself, not only for forgetting the purse in the first place, but for my so-called logic for not needing it.

Really? You thought of the phone and even the stupid chapstick, but not the key?

Well, I made it through the day, didn't I?

A lot of good that'll do you when you can't even get into your own house! And now you can't even call Mom either! It's not like you can just shrink yourself and creep under the door!

The last word I want to hear right now is 'shrink'—

My face twitches as a drop hits me. I open my eyes and watch as rain starts to fall. Not knowing what else to do, I sit on the top step, burying my head in my knees as I wrap my arms around them. The rain soaks me, but I don't care, since the dripping water and the biting cold distract me from any thoughts of what I've gone through today.

I'm not sure when or how long I doze off, but the next thing I know, I hear my name being called. I jolt awake, feeling stiff from the weather, and see Mom getting out of her car and hurrying toward me with heavy bags banging at her sides.

"Allie! What in the world are you doing out here?" she asks me with bewilderment.

Stretching my limbs and wiping wet hair from my eyes, I answer in annoyance, "Forgot my key."

"What? Speak up, Allie, I can't hear you."

"I forgot my key!"

Thunder rolls in the distance. Mom shakes her head, struggling to get the door open. ". . . here now. Allie . . . Allie! Help me, will you?"

Her voice penetrating my grumpy thoughts, I grab some of her bags and follow her inside. I shiver, grateful to be out of the cold. I take a shower while Mom puts away groceries and makes dinner. I come back down only to find that she won't be joining me because she has to go back to work. "I'm running late *again*," Mom mumbles in a panic, "Mr. Dean's really going to let me have it now." "Mom," I call, but she just shouts "Loveyoububhye" in one breath before literally running out the door. I stare at it after it shuts.

I just can't catch anything today, not even my own mother.

I trudge to the kitchen table and pick at the Italian meatloaf she left. Normally a favorite, now it just tastes like sawdust.

Later, I lounge on the couch, knowing that there's no point in forcing myself to do any homework since my brain will just mess it up if not reject it anyway. My roaming eyes fall on one of my DVDs, labeled with just my name. With feelings of nostalgia, I pop the disk out of its case and set it into the player. Images of my Kindergarten-self appear on the T.V. screen, along with my classmates from my Special Ed. sessions from eight years ago.

I watch with my chin on my knuckles as the other children and I, with the help of our teachers, dress up and act out old nursery rhymes. About ten minutes in, I get to "Humpty-Dumpty." Our star, made out of laminated paper cut-outs with cardboard bricks sandwiched in between, sits stable on the portable board "wall" until his "great fall." I'm not only one of the "king's men," but the one who pushes Humpty off the "wall," making him "shatter" on the floor. The other "king's man," a "horse," and I eagerly crawl over on the floor to fumble with the giant puzzle-like pieces. At one point, my fellow "king's man" tries to put Humpty's right side back on top of the wall first. I come over with his base crying out, "No! This one! This one goes first!"

Hearing myself sound so sensible like that compared to my then-classmates, I can't help but wonder how I could work out something so simple that these other kids couldn't, and then seem no different from them eight years later. Who am I, who seems to know more than the other kids with speech impediments (at least then), and yet babble like a baby now like they did? This comes less from pride than curiosity. I never had anything against those kids and I still don't. I don't remember them outside this footage, but I do know that they were my friends. Speech troubles hadn't meant anything to them so long as you were nice and wanted to play.

As I fall asleep later on, the memories comfort me and a part of me misses those days.

Ignorance really is bliss, isn't it?

~~~~~~~~~~~~~~

"Hey, honey," Mom says gently to me as I come into the kitchen the next morning.

"Hey," I say back.

Going back to her Instant Breakfast after we hug each other, she asks, "Are you ready to go?" It's Saturday, but we're both up early: Mom's going to work as usual while I'm going on a field trip.

"Yeah," I say with some hesitation as I eat my own breakfast, "except . . . my jacket . . . ."

"What about your jacket?" Reluctantly, I get it from the closet and show her the torn sleeve. "Oh, honey," she sighs. "What happened?"

"I think I outgrew it."

"Why didn't you say something last night?"

"How could I? You were gone!"

"What about before you showered?"

I clamp my mouth shut before I say something I'll regret later. A miserable silence follows. Eventually, I just say, "I'm sorry."

Mom pulls herself together. "Well, there's nothing we can do about it now. You can take my spare." She goes to the closet and pulls out her blue windbreaker. I try it on and I'm practically swimming in it. Mom tips her head sideways. (As if I didn't feel like a baby before.) Yet again, there seems to be something wrong about me at the wrong time.

On the other hand, I'd be lying if I said the jacket doesn't feel comfortable.

"Can you survive?" Mom asks in a tone both joking and apologetic. I nod, hoping to reassure her. She kisses me on the forehead. "Let's go."

~~~~~~~~~

Mom drives me to down to the dock by the river where my class is gathering. We are sailing for the whole day on a ferry called the *Wonder*. It's a nice-looking boat, but I don't think the name suits it. A name like the *Wonder* should go on a real ship, like a galleon.

Then again, it is *called a ferry.*
Yeah. So?
You know, like the magical creature.
Those aren't the same things at all and you know it!
Well, who says "ferry" and "fairy" aren't related somehow? People are changing word spellings and meanings all the time!
Arrgh, why do people have to be so complicated?

"Allie! Come on!" Mom is already halfway to the dock. I shift back to reality and get out of the car, running to catch up with her. We see my classmates surrounding Mrs. Heartred near the boat ramp.

"Alright, do you have everything?" Mom asks me.

"I think so."

"Books? Purse? Phone? Key?"

"Yes, yes," I keep telling her. I know she does this to help me, but again it doesn't feel right; she fusses whenever I don't need it, and never does when I do.

"Okay, then. I really hope you have a good time." I mutter "Me, too" and we embrace. "I'll be at the office today. Call me if you need anything." With one lass kiss, she leaves me. There's no real reason for it, but I instantly regret being alone as I watch Mom walk back into the car and drive away. With nothing else to do, I readjust my backpack and join the class.

I can't hear a word Mrs. Heartred is saying over all the noise of people rushing and equipment being lugged around, but I see her placing slips of paper in outstretched hands. Logic tells me those are our boat tickets. Knowing they must be important, whatever they are, I make my way to the front to get one. When Mrs. Heartred sees me, she lifts her head and looks at me as if I'm a weed that just sprouted up in her flower garden.

"Well, Allie," she says, "I'm glad to see you are paying some attention today."

"Yes, ma'am," I answer quietly, reaching out for a ticket.

She holds them back and probes me, "Yes, you are paying attention, or yes, you agree that I am glad?"

Say what?

"Uh . . . both? I mean, I'll try to pay attention. Obviously I can't know if you're glad or not, only you could know that. I mean, I *hope* you're glad . . . of course . . . ?" Realizing too late that I'm babbling again, I give Mrs. Heartred a crooked, hopeful smile.

Her expression is a mixture of disappointment and revulsion. She grudgingly holds out a ticket. I take it, dying to get away from her, but instead of letting go she keeps a firm grasp on it, making me nearly fall over backwards as I turn and try to leave. She looms over me with narrowed eyes saying, "Don't just say what you mean. Mean what you say. And please, try to *think* a bit before you do next time."

Not trusting myself to talk anymore, I just nod. When she finally lets me take my ticket, I hurry to the back of the group on wobbly legs. I hear some tittering behind me and look up to see the Decker sisters. I feel like a mouse in front of a bunch of lionesses. True to form, they approach me.

"It looks like the 'shrink' worked," Queenie comments, seeing me in Mom's jacket.

"Does this make her a little freak now, or an even bigger one?" Jackie wonders.

Asa answers with a cackle, "Either way, she looks like a mouse that got lost in a pool."

Queenie smirks. "In that case, how about we make her squeak like one?"

Jackie asks me with mock interest, "You *do* know what that means, right?"

"Or do we need to spell that out for you, too, little mouse?" says Asa.

The sisters circle me as they speak. I shudder and my mouth dries up, making it hard to swallow. But before anything else can happen, Mrs. Heartred calls out, "Alright, everyone! It's time to get on board! Be sure to have your tickets ready!"

Feeling grateful to my teacher for once, I slide into the line of classmates, making sure that there are a lot of people between me and the sisters. Just then, a camera flashes behind me. I turn around, but the boy behind me shouts "Hey!" as he walks into me. "Sorry," I say to him politely. I shove the incident out of my mind as one by one we all hand the boat employee our tickets and walk up the ramp onto the ferry. Not long after, the foghorn bellows and we drift out onto the river.

I wish I could watch the receding of the dock longer, but Mrs. Heartred calls us together again, forcing me to turn and listen. I have to strain to hear her with all the other passengers chatting and bustling past us.

"Alright, then . . . you know we . . . poetry next . . . The object . . . this trip . . .

inspiration. You are . . . move about, observe . . . take notes . . ."

I take a chance with the girl next to me. "So we're using this boat ride to get ideas for poetry?" Hearing her "Yes," I quickly thank her and try to refocus on Mrs. Heartred, but I can't help thinking, *Okay, I think this makes sense, but shouldn't we have studied some basics or something first so we actually know what we're doing?*

As if she had heard me speaking aloud, Mrs. Heartred's voice seems to be almost on top of me: "The reason I am assigning this before we officially begin the poetry unit is so that I can see what you all can do *without* professional influence." Our eyes meet, and a lump forms in my throat. "We will meet in the dining room for lunch at twelve o'clock sharp. Come or go hungry. By about four o'clock we should be nearing the dock, so make sure to have your things on your person by then and gather where we are now. Remember, we are here for educational purposes. I will know how attentive you are by the quality of your work, so I suggest that you *do not dally.* Understood?" We all murmur and nod. "Alright then, you are dismissed."

The class scatters. After walking to the other end of the boat and looking around, I lean against a wall and rest my eyes, sighing with relief. Maybe now I can get a little peace and quiet.

But before I can start to relax, another flash pierces through my eyelids, making me flinch. I open my eyes just in time to see someone aiming a camera at me. I move toward him. I can't see his face because of the camera, but he shifts it just enough to see me coming, then runs the other way. I go after him.

Why would anyone want to take pictures of me?

Maybe he was aiming at something behind you?

I see him leave the deck and enter the ferry's interior. I keep an eye on the doorway he uses and cross the threshold. I don't see him. Discouraged, I head back outside. But then, I hear the camera snap and I see the weird photographer at my left, this time much closer. "Hey!" I call out. I hear him laugh as he dashes away. I can't believe how fast he is. I chase him in and out of the ferry's interior, but after only a few minutes, he escapes again.

Now irritated, I stop to catch my breath. Resolving not to chase him and make a fool of myself again if I see or hear a camera near me, I thrust my hands in my pockets and walk around. The sound of other kids talking reaches my ears. I see a small group, some sitting on benches, others standing or resting against a wall or rail. In spite of myself, I listen.

"How does she get so dirty that often?" a boy asks a girl on a bench.

"Well, the fact that she's so hairy doesn't help," she responds to him.

I speak up without thinking, "So is Harry just the type of guy who just likes to get dirty?"

Everyone gives me an odd look. The girl asks me, "Who's Harry? I was talking about my dog, Dinah." I feel my face heat up, but before I can say anything, she stands up. "Listen, guys, I'm getting thirsty. Why don't we get something to drink?"

Everyone walks past me like I'm not there. I catch snippets of talk as they drift around me. "That sounds like fun!" "So, do you want to go?" "Sorry, but I have to go and get some floss for my class project after school that day . . ."

"Oh," I try again, "do you sew, too? I love cross-stitching! I just got this beautiful shade of red for a Welsh Dragon piece I've been working on . . ." I trail off because everyone is now staring at me with cocked eyebrows and open mouths.

"You sew with dental floss?" the girl from before says.

Oh, crap.

"Uh, no . . . I-I meant the, uh . . . it's a special kind of thread—"

"Duh," I hear Asa's sly voice right behind me. "How else would you get it into your teeth?" I wince as I turn around to see the Deckers cutting off my escape route once again.

"Sewing with dental floss," Queenie muses. "That's quite the hobby you have, mouse."

"Do you use tooth picks and toilet paper for needles and cloth, too?" Jackie teases.

"Then she'd be more like a rat than a mouse!" Asa laughs outright.

"That's right," Queenie purrs at me, "a slinking, sniveling, spineless little rat."

Eyes stinging with tears and face burning with shame, I run away, this time not caring where I go or who I ram into as long as it means solitude in the end. I make it to the bow of the ferry, lean over the rail, and bury my face in my arms.

Why? Why the hell do I even bother?

"Are you crying?"

I jump in alarm. There is a man next to me. He looks like he's in his late twenties or early thirties, and he is wearing the thickest pair of glasses I've ever seen, making his eyes look huge. His front teeth poke out from the upper jaw of his thin face and his light hair lies in flat heaps as it reaches past his long, skinny ears, making him appear almost rabbit-like. More importantly, his speech doesn't seem right somehow, as if he's only just learned how to speak despite his age (not that I'm one to talk). I can tell by his accent, though, that he's British. It reminds me of European nobility, but that image fades, and not only because of his speech. He stares at me with a gleam in his eye I'm not sure I like.

"What?" I say.

"You *are* crying, aren't you?" he asks. *He sounds as if he* wants *me to be crying.*

"No," I answer, looking away from him.

"Oh, how unfortunate."

I turn back sharply. *Did I hear that right?* I think before asking, "What did you say?"

"I said that is unfortunate."
So I'm not being slow this time.
"Why?"

"Because you asked me what I just said," he replies.

"What? No, I mean, why is it unfortunate that I'm not crying?"

"Oh, that. Well, you see, Miss, I happen to be most fluent in crying, as well as sobbing, sniffling, coughing, and even headache, sore throat and stuffy nose!"[1]

"Headache . . ." I echo blankly.

He grins and nods, adding as he shakes a finger at me, "*I* had a *classical* education."

I realize that this is not my APD messing with my brain again; this guy really is mentally ill. Besides the way he speaks, his manner seems . . . childish. I can't think of any other word for it. Now he's gazing at me like an eager puppy.

"You're kidding . . . right?" I ask with some caution.

His smile disappears. "Of course not, you silly! I'm not a lady *or* a goat!"

It takes me several seconds to grasp what he means by this, and when I do, I'm disgusted as well as angry. As if I don't have a hard enough time with *normal* people, now I have to take the same crap from a guy who has the I.Q. of a three-year-old?

Or is it five-year-old? When do kids start talking again?

I shake my head to stop another mental argument. "I don't have time for this," I mutter.

The man puts a hand to his chin in thoughtful seriousness. "That is also unfortunate, but then, Time *is* a very busy man. Twenty-four-hour day and all that, you know."

Fed up, I storm off.

"Oy, wait!" I hear him call out. "Come back!"

His voice sounds so distressed that I stop and face him again. My eye catches an object hidden in his hands: a digital camera. I look the man up and down and full in the face and, yet again, I feel like kicking myself. I *knew* I wasn't imagining it. *This* is the guy responsible for all those flashes and the one I've been chasing all over this stupid boat. More furious than ever, I stride over and snatch the camera out of the man's hands.

"Oh, no, no, stop, don't do that!" he begs me. "Please, don't hurt them!"

I stop, feeling like a bully taking a toy from a toddler. *Why am I doing this?* Sure, I can be emotional when I'm frustrated, but I've never lashed out at anyone like this before, let alone someone with a mental disability. Like me. I feel ashamed of myself as I return the camera to the man, and even more so as I watch him hug it like a teddy bear.

After about a minute of this, he looks back up at me as if I'm a friend who hadn't just taken a precious possession of his. "Do you want to see my girls?" he asks.

Before I can respond, he shoves the camera in my face, making me have to push it back so I can see the screen properly. My surprise gives way to fascination. Each photo I click through features at least one girl, some my age, others even younger, running at parks, dancing in yards, playing with toys or friends, eating snacks and grinning with messy faces. They really are adorable. If I didn't know whose camera this is, I'd have thought that these were done by a pro.

"Aren't they lovely?" He says as if gazing upon a sacred treasure.

I nod, unable to take my eyes away. I'm wondering why there are no adults or even boys in the pictures when I gasp at the most recent addition in his album: me.

"She's a personal favorite of mine," he remarks in a dreamy voice. "That long blue coat of hers makes her look like a beautiful little queen, gazing out at her kingdom . . ."

"You think I'm beautiful?" I blurt out.

He gives me a hard look. "What on earth do you mean by that? I was talking about *her*, not *you*."

"But that *is* me in the picture," I protest after a moment of stunned silence.

"She's not a 'that,' she's a 'she,'" he counters. "And *she* is *her*, not *you*."

I try to explain, "No, I meant the girl in the picture is me—" but he cuts me off.

"Stuff and nonsense! *She* is *her* in *there*"—he jabs a finger at the screen and then at me—"and *you* are *you* out *here*!

"Who *are* you, anyway?"[2]

My mouth drops open at the question. "Oh, uh . . . my name is Allie."

"That's nice, but *who* are *you*?"

"I just said—"

"You did? What do you mean? *Explain yourself!*"

My anxiety returns at his commanding tone. "Well, I . . . uh . . ."

"Wrong from start to finish!" he cuts me off again.

I flounder in my cluttered brain before demanding, "Well, who are *you*?"

"Charlie!"

We both jump. A woman is coming toward us in a determined march. The man hides the camera guiltily behind his back, quivering like a child who's just gotten caught doing something naughty by his mother. She doesn't look old enough to be his mother, but she may as well be the way she scolds him.

"Charlie! I've been searching everywhere for you! How many times have I told you not to speak to strangers?"

"I'm s-s-sorry, Lily . . ." He hangs his head, looking like he's about to burst into tears. Hearing him stutter like that shocks me. *He must be terrified of her,* I think with pity.

The woman turns to me. "I'm sorry, child. Has my brother been bothering you?"

Yes. Wait. "Brother"?

"I w-wasn't doing n-n-n-nothing wrong this time, Lily, I s-s-swear!" the man stammers.

"Never mind, never mind," she tells him impatiently. To me she repeats, "You're sure you're alright?" I nod, just wanting to get out of the situation. She eyes me for one more uncomfortable moment before going back to the man's pleas, which are getting annoying. "Alright, Charlie, please calm down. I'm not that upset. I wanted to find you because it's lunch time." With motherly temptation now in her voice, she adds, "There is soup being served in the dining room now."

I can't believe his change of emotion. "Beautiful soup?" he asks like it's the best Christmas present ever.

"Yes, Charlie, lots of beautiful soup. Why don't we get some before it gets cold, hmm?"

"BEAUUUTIFUL SOOOUP!" he sings out, making several people stop and look our way. I cringe.

"Charlie!" the woman says firmly. "Behave yourself, or you'll get no soup. Understand?"

"Oh, yes, Lily, yes." He cocks his head as if listening to something. "Do you hear that?" he whispers. "I hear the soup calling. It is saying 'Drink me. Please come drink me.'"

"Well, then, let's not keep it waiting. Come along, Charlie."[4]

I watch as he is led by the hand (staggering somewhat) to the other side of the boat. I'm completely at a loss as to what just happened, but I don't have time to dwell on it. The woman's comment reminds me that I also have to go to lunch.

After an agonizing meal next to Queenie ("This is really quite charming. It will be like a nice vacation before *all* that extra work I have to do later"), I go back outside. I sit down in one of the deck chairs, take my bottle of water out of my backpack, and start drinking.

"What are you doing?"

Startled, I choke on my water. After coughing and clearing my throat, I turn to see Charlie grinning in the chair next to me.

Jeez, what does this guy want?

"Shouldn't you be with your sister?" I ask him.

"Oh, we're playing hide and seek."

He says this like it's the most natural thing in the world, but I'm certain that it isn't the case. I feel a little afraid now, both to get him worked up by forcing him to come with me and to be with him at all. I decide, or rather pray, that the best thing to do is keep him occupied until Lily comes around again. I mean, the ferry's not *that* big.

"What are you doing?" he repeats more loudly, obviously not intending to go anywhere.

"Oh, uh, nothing," I answer with awkward slowness.

Charlie looks baffled. "But you're doing lots of things, aren't you? You're sitting, you're drinking, oh, and you're breathing, and talking—oh wait, you're not talking now, are you? But you *were* just now—"

"Alright, I get it," I interrupt. Somehow, it doesn't bother me much to do so with him. "If you know that much already, why did you bother to ask?"

"I want a story," Charlie announces. I grumble as he gazes out at the glittering water. "I always love a good story on a golden afternoon such as this."

"Believe me. This whole day has been *anything* but golden."

"Why?" He looks around. "Have you seen other colors today?"

Aw, screw it.

"Try the stormy grey that makes you want to cry for hours, the pitch black that blinds you and makes you stumble, or the kind of multicolor that's supposed to look cool but just gives you massive headaches . . . instead . . ." I trail off in increasing astonishment.

"Yes! Yes! I've seen those, too! I told you I spoke crying and headache, didn't I?"

I barely hear him, only this time it's because I can't believe what I've just said.

That was . . . awesome.
No kidding.
Did I really just say those words?
Yeah! That, my friend, is poetry!

I'm smiling to myself at my verbal triumph when Charlie grabs my hand, positively beaming. "I knew it!"

"Knew what?" I say with deep suspicion.

"I knew you were a good mad!"

Completely taken aback, I feel insulted at first, but that diminishes as I watch Charlie's face. Mental illness or not, it seems sincere. Plus, it does feel good to have someone listen to me say something nonsensical and *not* judge me for a change. Without pulling my hand away, I ask, "What's that supposed to mean?"

"I know you're mad because you talk to me."

Oookaaay.

"What about your sister? Lily, right? She talks to you, doesn't she?"

Charlie shakes his head. "Lily doesn't like me because she's a not-mad and I'm a bad mad. But you, you're a good mad because you talk to me and you're nice to me."

"There's no such thing as a 'good mad.'" My tone is sharper than I would like, but I want him to understand. "I *do* have a sort of 'madness' if that's what you want to call it, but it's not so much that I do bad things as I don't do anything people want at all! I mean, people might as well be asking me 'Why is an alligator like an icebox'[5] for all I know—"

"Oh, that's easy," Charlie breaks in, "because their insides need to live." I stare, but he doesn't seem to notice as he explains. "Iceboxes keep food cold, and alligators have cold blood. The food and the blood are the insides, you see, and it's that frosty cold that keeps those insides good until they can be warmed up nice and cozy again. Simple."

Wow.

"That's really impressive, Charlie," I say, meaning it. "I never would have guessed that."

"Really?" He seems astonished.

I nod. I know it isn't logical, but it sure is more fun.

"Oh, Time spared a moment for me after all," Charlie cries happily. "Time is a very busy man, you know, but once in a while he'll find it in his schedule to help a useless fool like me."

"You're *not* useless, and you're *not* a fool," I tell him.

"Oh, but I am," Charlie replies. "It is because I am my mother's punishment."

I jerk my hand out of his in surprise. He's so serious now, not in his immature way but like a real adult recalling a powerful dream. Or memory.

"A long, long time ago," he begins, "I lived among the fairies. We did nothing but play and revel in each other's madness. They are all good mads, too, you understand. Even

34

Time himself leaves them alone, so they can sing and race and have as much tea as they like all day long. It was wonderful.

"But one day, my mother did something terrible. She insulted Lady Mercury. She danced the 'Lobster Quadrille,' which the Lady found utterly offensive. Even worse, Mother ate the water people, everything from whiting to mock turtle. Then she wore a hat in the shape of a fish, a goldfish, no less. As punishment, Lady Mercury sent her messenger to my mother with a curse.

"I began to grow. I grew and I grew until I became too large to fit in the fairy realm anymore and was forced to go and live in the human world. Humans don't like mad people the way fairies do. It was not too bad at first. I had my lovely Lily, who was a good mad then. But as I grew even more, she became a not-mad, like Mother and Father and everyone else. When I was smaller it made Lily and Mother and Father laugh when I would get leaves or straw in my hair.[6] But now if I do that, they call me filthy and become upset."

As he speaks, his voice low and forlorn, I remember my own father arguing with Mom in front of me when I was six. My eyes dampen. I still don't know all the reasons behind their divorce, but I've always

35

wondered whether it had anything to do with my disorder.

Charlie puts a hand to his chest as he continues. "The only friend I've had is my little bread-and-butterfly.[7] He managed to escape from the fairy realm to be with me. A cheery little soul, he is, but like all fairy folk, so flighty and fidgety. I do love him so, but I don't like it when he gets *too* fidgety because then he could blow my candle out by mistake."

I wipe my eyes, trying to understand this.

His candle?

"Well, now, what do we have here?" I swivel in my chair and see Queenie, holding an elbow in one hand and her cheek in the other. "Strange company you're keeping, though I can't say I'm entirely surprised."

I freeze, my mind fluttering like its own butterfly. Just then, I hear severe coughing and snorting behind me. I whip back around to find Charlie doubled over in his chair clutching his chest. I slap him on the back and to my huge relief, he starts to breathe normally again.

"The cake told me to eat it," he croaks. "I was only doing what it commanded."

"What the cake wha—" That's when I notice a half-eaten cupcake on the deck floor. I go to it and pick it up, making out some letters sprinkled with something gray on the pink frosting:

AT

E

I blink.

"EAT ME"?

Curious, I sniff the cupcake—and then drop it as I begin sneezing. "Pepper!" The shock forces the word from my throat. I then hear laughter coming from Jackie and Asa, who are standing haughtily beside a sick-looking Charlie.

"Looks like freaks of a feather sneeze together," Jackie says once she recovers.

"Oh, sorry," Asa says, pretending to be sympathetic. "Was that too obscure for you?"

"You *gave* Charlie this?" I demand angrily, pointing to the splattered, broken cupcake. "You put pepper on it and actually let him *eat* it?"

Jackie shrugs, saying with infuriating reasonableness, "Hey, it's just like he said. He was doing what the cake commanded."

Queenie's gaze criticizes me. "Are you accusing us?" she asks.

My resolve wavers as her eyes bore into my own.

"Did my sisters *say* they gave him the cupcake? Did you *see* them do it, with your own two eyes?"

Her voice is so convincing, so sure . . . so dangerous . . . I can't fight it. I'm about to shake my head, cursing my conscience, when Charlie speaks up:

"Is there going to be a party?"

The sisters and I all stare at him; his brightness seems so out-of-place right now, especially since he was just gasping for air a moment ago.

"Oh, I do so love parties," Charlie giggles, clapping his hands with glee. "Will there be flamingo mallets and hedgehog balls for croquet? I particularly love the parties with costumes! You girls' costumes are so funny! You look like a pack of cards!"

The sisters' faces redden at this, but Charlie's words drown them out in my mind.

He's right. They do look . . . Wait a second. Queenie? Jackie? Asa? Decker?

I feel my lips being pulled into a smile. Then I chuckle. Before I know it, I'm laughing along with Charlie. I laugh even harder when I see the sisters gape at us like fish.

"WHAT IS GOING ON HERE?"

"Allie and this guy are making fun of us, Mrs. Heartred!" Jackie shouts.

My laughter dies out as our teacher approaches us like she's on a warpath.

"Allie Little! What, pray tell, do you find so amusing about your fellow students? And *who* is this man?"

Seeing Mrs. Heartred makes Charlie even more excited. He tugs at my sleeve from behind me, saying, "Oooh! Oooh! Is that supposed to be the knave?"

Mrs. Heartred's eyes nearly pop out of their sockets. "I *beg* your pardon?"

As fast as it had gone, my laughter returns stronger than ever. But I manage to sputter my words out: "It's true! You four are *so* ridiculous!"

"*What did you say, young lady?!*" Mrs. Heartred says, more outraged than ever.

I calm down and look her right in the eye. "You heard me." My humor gone now, I approach her, the sisters huddled around her. (I'm thrilled to see none of them are smiling.) I'm vaguely aware of some classmates and other passengers starting to gather around us, but I pay no attention to them. I'm amazed at my own confidence, which seems to grow with each step I take. As a matter of fact, the sisters seem to be shrinking as I get closer. I feel like I tower over them as I say, "Was *that* too obscure for you?"

Mrs. Heartred's face is now purple, her gasps turning into shrieks. "That does it! First, you get lazy in my class, whining about your 'Auditory Processing' nonsense, and now you make friends with this *beastly* man and cause God knows what kind of trouble! You are a stupid, selfish, spoiled little brat! I'll have you expelled for this! Do you hear me? *Expelled!!!*"

"I don't freaking care!" I explode back. "I'm *sick* of your one-sided lectures, I'm *sick* of your psycho-bullying, and I'm *especially sick* of you treating me like I'm a coward and an idiot! I may not understand everything I see and hear, but I'm not stupid, and neither is Charlie!"

I glance back at him watching us. He looks puzzled, yet pleased.

"What are you gawking at, freak?" Queenie snarls at him.

"*Shut up, you!!!*" I yell in her face. "You're the only freaks around here! You look like a pack of cards and you act like a pack of rotten *bitches!*"

These words are barely out of my mouth when all three Deckers lunge at me. My body is smashed against a wall, shaken and jerked around by punches, scratches, and kicks. Then they stop and I slump to the floor. Something hot and wet runs down my face. I can't see . . . I feel so . . . dizzy . . .

Where are all those voices coming from? Why are they so loud?

"Someone . . . help . . . !"

". . . Lily! . . . candle . . . going . . ."

"Charlie . . . don't!"

Who is that? A lady?

40

What about Charlie? Where is he? Is he alright?

Will someone please stop that screaming . . . it hurts . . . please . . . don't hurt . . .

~~~~~~~~~~

Finally, I see the castle!

To my surprise, however, I see the tuxedoed white rabbit bounding toward me. Once we reach each other, without either of us stopping, he makes a sharp turn and speeds on beside me.

"Oh, won't they be savage if they've been kept waiting!" he moans.

"Who?" I puff out. "The queen?"

"Certainly not! I mean the fairies!" *Without slowing his pace the rabbit leaps into the air with a graceful twirl that makes me smile in awe.* "I simply must remember to thank Master Time for his great generosity! The curse is broken at last! That wretched queen is gone now and I have found the fairies! Oh, I can hardly wait to see them again!"

"That's great!" *I reply, confused but still happy for him.*

"I do wish you could come with me," *the rabbit says with regret in his voice.*

"What? But why can't I?" *I cry with dismay as I realize I want to go, too.*

"Because my candle has burned out!"

"What in the world does that mean?"

"Come, we mustn't dawdle," the rabbit urges me, "or we shall both be late!"

"But what does it matter to me now? Why am I still running?"

"Because *your* candle hasn't burned out yet, but it might if we don't hurry!"

"Wha—" I don't have any more air in my lungs to talk. My legs are burning, yet they still won't listen to my plea to stop.

Even so, the rabbit grabs my arm as if he means to drag me along. "Please tell my Lily I love her!" he begs me. "And don't you worry, you'll be back, I wager. After all, you're just as wonderfully mad as the rest of us!"

With that, he spins me around with incredible strength and then literally throws me into a hole that has just appeared in the sky above us. As I fall—or is it fly?—I hear the rabbit's last words: "Fly like a bat and twinkle like a tea tray, my little dormouse!"

I scream as I'm shot upwards, tossing and turning every which way until I feel sick . . .

I yelp as my body freezes, not only in mid-air, but as in every part of me. I start to panic as I realize I can't even move my eyes, though I see a light with huge shadows on each side of me. I also find that my ears are catching sounds as well.

". . . eyes . . . hear me . . . why . . . wake up . . .

I know that voice.

Come on, why can't I move?

Using all my strength, I move my eyelids; I'm startled to learn that my eyes have already been open for a while.

When did I open my eyes?

". . . God . . . Allie . . . can you hear . . . ?"

Finally, I'm able to blink . . . and the shadows become clear.

"Mom?" My voice sounds so raspy.

"Allie! Oh, thank God, Allie, you're awake!" Mom wails, grasping my hand and putting it to her face. Her eyes are red and puffy . . . from crying?

I'm even more confused when I see that I'm in a bed that isn't mine. "What—ooowww," I groan. Pain rips through my body when I try to sit up. There's a skinny tube in my arm, my skin is red, purple, and yellow with bruises and scratches, and my face feels like it's been shredded.

"Don't move," Mom orders me. "You're in the hospital. You've been unconscious for four days. Amelia's here, too. She told me everything."

Another woman emerges into my view.

"Lily!" I exclaim.

"Welcome back, Allie," she says. "It's about time we were properly introduced."

43

"I still can't believe it," Mom says with furious disbelief. "How the *hell* could the school let this happen?" She looks at me again. "Why didn't you tell me you were being bullied?"

I try to think of how to answer when I notice a table nearby, covered with flowers, get-well cards, boxes of candy, and a huge, stuffed, white rabbit in a suit with a little fake pocket watch stitched into its paw.

'   "Those are from your classmates," Lily explains.

The rabbit . . . Charlie!

"Lily, where's Charlie?" I ask. "Is he here, too?"

"Allie," Mom tries to calm me. "Take it easy, now."

Lily's face falls. She closes her eyes and takes a deep breath but doesn't reply, her shoulders slumping as if she's tired. My heart plummets into my stomach. I almost wish my APD kept me from understanding what Lily isn't saying.

"His candle *was* blown out," I whisper to myself.

Both women looked stunned.

"Allie! That's a terrible thing to say!" Mom scolds me. "Unless . . ." Terror clouds her face. "Oh, Jesus, I hope this isn't something worse than your APD."

44

"How do you know about the candle?" Lily asks in a small voice. "And what is APD?"

"Mom, it's okay, I'm fine," I tell her. "Will you let me talk?"

She nods slowly, still uneasy. But neither she nor Lily interrupts me as I talk about my disorder and my time with Charlie on the *Wonder*. For whatever reason, every word flows out, and I don't digress or babble as usual. I even talk about my dream. Somehow, it just feels like a good idea . . . until I finish and see Lily staring at me with a strange expression.

Finally, she speaks, looking down at her feet, her voice shaking. "I've looked after Charlie since our parents passed away. Our mother . . . she had a passion for sea life. She especially loved seafood. It was always her favorite. There was nothing wrong with her during her pregnancy with Charlie so far as Father and I could tell, but it wasn't until just before his birth that we learned that the fish Mother was eating had been contaminated with mercury."

A hand flies to Mom's mouth.

"Holy . . ." I'm unable to finish the sentence.

"Charlie was born prematurely," Lily goes on, "and besides his mental capacity, his heart was affected as well. It was very weak.[8] I made up the butterfly/candle story to make him understand why he couldn't eat certain foods or get so flustered. Sometimes he'd want so badly to play with people, especially children, that he'd get worked up and become a nuisance. Other times he'd become so terrified around adults that he'd cling to me when we were outside, or refuse to leave his room for days. Still, I decided to chance bringing Charlie on a vacation to America so he wouldn't feel as cooped up as he was back home in England. But I had no idea how much he really understood what was wrong with him. I don't know if it was the noise or the panic, or the shock of seeing you beaten like that . . . his heart just couldn't . . ." Her breath trembles. She pauses to compose herself before lifting a sad smiling face at me.

"I lost sight of Charlie again after lunch and was looking everywhere for him on the *Wonder*. I eventually found him with you. I watched you defend him and yourself, as did the other passengers. Truly magnificent. Your classmates were also impressed, and horrified when those sisters attacked you. Apparently they all hated Mrs. Heartred as well, but were too afraid to say or do anything about it. But don't worry, dear. That vile woman is never going to torment a child or anyone else ever again, and neither are those horrible girls."

I'm so overwhelmed I don't respond. Lily gives me an understanding pat on my hand.

46

"Perhaps the reason Charlie took such a fancy to you was because he believed you are a bit like him."

"A good mad," I reply softly.

Tears run down Mom's cheeks. "I'm so sorry, honey." She strokes my hair. "And I'm sorry for your brother, too," she tells Lily.

"In my dream, he told me to say he loves you, Lily," I say. It sounds ridiculous when I say it out loud, but I feel like I should offer her something, anything.

Lily dabs at her eyes with a handkerchief. "Thank you, Mrs. Little. And thank *you*, Allie, for your kindness and for making my brother's final moments on earth less lonesome. I'm glad he's now where he feels happiest"—she chuckles—"even if it is among the mad."

~~~~~~~~~~~

We all talk some more until evening when a doctor stops by. He's happy to see that I'm awake and alert, and announces, to all our relief, that there are no abnormalities and I'll heal just fine, though he wants me to stay a bit longer just in case. After he asks that I be left alone to rest and then leaves, Lily tells us she has to go and get Charlie's body back to England. She gives me her contact information, as well as the pictures Charlie took of me, waiting in line to get on the *Wonder*, resting my eyes as I lean against the wall, and looking out at the tree-covered land across the river.

"I was always trying to tell Charlie to stop with his photography as I was afraid of what would happen if anyone found them and what they would think." She smiles at me with regret. "I wish I'd seen sooner what an innocent and lovely vision he had."[9]

All I can do is nod.

Mom brings over the stuffed rabbit and, at my request, lends me her pen and some notebook paper. She gives me a worried frown, but I promise her I won't wear myself out.

Once I'm alone in the room, I watch the sun set outside the window and think about all that's happened. The initial shock has worn off, and somehow I can't bring myself to cry or even feel too sad. It's weird, but I can't help thinking of Charlie as if he himself was a dream: a source of fond childish memories, an impossibility in the here-and-now, an entity seen and known once and never again. I smile as I realize that that's how I want to remember him.

I take my new rabbit in both hands and look into his big blue eyes. "What say you, lad," I say to him in playful British. "Will you revel in a little madness with me?"

It's probably the last rays of the sun, but I prefer to think that the rabbit really hears me as his eyes flash and wink. With my arm around him, I ease myself up a bit, place the paper in my lap, and put the pen tip to it. I command my hand, and this time, it listens.

"Who Are You? Explain Yourself!" A Guide to Allie's Adventure on the Wonder

Aside from the bizarre creatures and enchanted treats, a crucial aspect of the theme of madness in *Alice's Adventures in Wonderland* is its use of language. Some of the story's appeal comes from the inhabitants' butchering of words, but Alice's unsuccessful attempts to decipher the resulting absurd logic causes her great distress. The titular character of *Allie's Adventure on the Wonder* is likewise caught in a sort of real-life Wonderland, thwarted by an inability to comprehend what is being said around her because of a condition called Auditory Processing Disorder (APD). The Duchess, "fond . . . of finding morals in things," (Carroll 130) believes she is teaching Alice about life, but her "morals" are ridiculous and make almost no sense. Allie's Special Ed. Advisor, Mrs. Dutch, similarly uses idioms to encourage Allie to learn from her experiences. But the phrase "Whatever doesn't kill you makes you stronger," for example, sounds to Allie like "Whatever does kill you makes you sunder" (Adams). Ironically, Charlie's fantastic, though impaired, thinking, such as his distinction between "a good mad" and "a bad mad," helps Allie as she copes with her condition. Neither Alice nor her creator, Lewis Carroll (Charles Lutwidge Dodgson), had APD or any related disorder, yet the way they portray aspects of it in their use—or misuse—of words influences how these characters see themselves and are seen by others.

Defined in one sense as "the auditory equivalent of dyslexia" (Bellis i), Auditory Processing Disorder affects the way the brain takes in and interprets sounds, though the physical structure and function of the ear may be, and often is, normal. Despite the name, APD also impacts visual and social learning. One of Alice's biggest disadvantages in Wonderland is that she involves herself in situations when she "ought to have wondered" (Carroll 63) the full scope of the consequences. She eats the "EAT ME" cake believing she will be able to "reach the key" or "creep under the door" (69) to the garden depending on the resulting size change. In all probability, however, she would end up being too large to fit through the door again—as is proven in the following chapter—or much too small to get very far or properly enjoy the garden. Allie reasons that she "can manage without [her purse]" (Adams) as long as she does not need anything in it; but she recalls too late that her house key is also in her purse. In both cases, the logic's purpose is defeated and both girls are left with no way of moving forward.

The function of any key is to enable one to pass a barrier of some kind. In light of this lack of a "key" to good judgment, Allie and Alice are both painfully aware—even to the point of tears—of how in real life, "greater emphasis is placed on [academic] skills . . . than on the more creative abilities that show cognitive processes related to abstract thought and mental flexibility" (Bellis 87). Alice despairs in reciting "*the little crocodile*" instead of "*the little busy bee*" (Carroll 73) when trying to recall her lessons, and Allie panics when trying to proofread Queenie's book report on *The Hobbit*. Because "so much time and effort may be spent trying to decode each letter, each word," the overall topic becomes lost and forgotten (Bellis 45). Language is one of the foundations of human interaction, communication, and development; the difficulty or inability of APD sufferers to utilize it can leave them feeling increasingly isolated and discouraged.

As a story that prides itself on nonsense, *Alice in Wonderland* provides numerous examples of "language as play" (Kelly 23), mocking its literalities and liabilities. But for those whose ability to communicate effectively is impaired, this can be anything but fun. Applying to real people as much as to Alice and Allie, "[to] wield language . . . be it intelligible, 'normal,' or otherwise, is to have the power to define, to create, and to destroy. When language ceases, so does existence" (Turner 244). Alice mistakes "tale" for "tail" and "not" for "knot" as the mouse gives his "dry" lecture. He feels "[insulted] by [her] talking such nonsense" (Carroll 82-4) and walks away never to return. The other animals do the same when she very thoughtlessly talks about her cat. Allie also baffles her audience when she asks questions about a "guy" named "Harry" when the discussion is about a "hairy" (Adams) dog named Dinah. Her classmates start to leave, stopping only to stare at Allie when she inadvertently claims to "sew with dental floss." The girls' speeches "[cause] a remarkable sensation," (Carroll 84) and as a result, the parties "all [move] off" and the girls "[are] soon left alone."

The imagery of burning candles—introduced by Alice when she shrinks for the first time—symbolizes smallness and death intertwined. In her first dream, Allie encounters creatures who want her to stay and "play" with them, but she "[flares] up" (Adams) just in time to return to waking life. Charlie's comparable interpretation of a candle as a veil between himself and the realm of fairies (traditionally small and sometimes overactive creatures very much like Carroll's) is indicative of separate realities, namely those of the mind and of the afterlife. Allie's stand against Mrs. Heartred and the Decker sisters, as well as Charlie's death, not only coincides with Alice's stand against the Queen of Hearts and the domineering qualities of Wonderland, but emphasizes the main characters' unstable dreamlike existence[10] because of the mind's "tension between . . . [the] expectations and . . . the actuality" of real life (Kelly 19).

In a similar vein to "Carroll's own fundamental duality" (17), Allie and Alice share characteristics of a "disembodied intellect" (16). Whenever they are not being emotional due to their misunderstandings, they are reacting with a "quiet, detached interest" (28), passive to the point of seeming unfeeling. Alice and Allie let few single thoughts linger very long in their minds and endure what they do less out of determination than out of simple acceptance.[11] The Duchess' baby turns into a pig right in Alice's arms, yet she calmly sets it down and watches it wander off, and Allie has few (awkward) opinions regarding Charlie's digital photos of young girls and in fact admires them.[12] The relationships between Allie, Charlie, and his sister, Lily, reflect certain factors of the mindset of Lewis Carroll. Just as neither Allie nor Lily can say that they had ever really known or understood Charlie, there is even now a "potent mythology surrounding the name 'Lewis Carroll,' rather than the reality of the man, Charles Dodgson" (Leach 9). In spite of their difficulties with words, Allie desires to write stories and write them well, while Charlie creates fantasies in order to better grasp his own situation in life. Many people with speech/auditory disabilities can be very creative, and Carroll, "like many creative people . . . needed certain conditions" (Woolf 213-4) for both his writing and his affiliations. Like Charlie and Allie, Carroll "disliked outsiders poking their nose into the informal, friendly little world he created" (218). (Depending on the exact nature and severity of the condition, APD patients may require one-on-one interaction or time alone in quieter environments to perform at their best.)

Each story illustrates how these characters must continually make their way throughout "a world made up of contradictions" (Kelly 15). The girls' increasing loneliness, along with their youthful but compromised mindset, generates for them imaginary friends of sorts—or rather enemies. Alice is "very fond of pretending to be two people" (Carroll 68), but as charming as this may sound, this habit of talking to herself tends to cause more harm than good as she often "[scolds] herself" with comments like "Come, there's no use in crying like that!"; "You ought to be ashamed of yourself" (71); and "Oh, you foolish Alice!" (87). Allie also engages in harsh mental arguments, calling herself and her own ideas "stupid," then telling her inner voice to "*Shut up!*" (Adams). Charlie's claim of Allie's madness by her friendly association with him, hence his labeling of her as "a good mad," parallels the Cheshire Cat's presentation of an ironically "*logical* argument to prove his assertion" (Turner 248) that Alice "must be [mad] . . . or [she] wouldn't have come [to Wonderland]" (Carroll 110). People with APD may "spend hours agonizing over possible hidden meanings that might be buried in day-to-day communications" with others because they know their "perception may not always be representative of reality" (Bellis xxi).

Time is yet another crucial factor in the way these characters think. Both Charlie and the Mad Hatter claim to be acquainted with Time, acknowledging it as a personified entity. Charlie considers Time to be "a very busy man" (Adams), and the Hatter firmly tells Alice "[if she] knew Time as well as [he does] . . . [she] wouldn't talk about wasting [him]" (Carroll 115). Both heroines have some awareness of this, albeit in a more practical sense. Alice, for instance, must find a way to shrink herself out of the White

Rabbit's house before the animals "burn the house down" (Carroll 90), as well as take the baby away from the Duchess and the cook as they are "sure to kill it in a day or two" (107) with their frenzied carelessness. Allie tries (but fails) to get her book report done on time and to get out from under Mrs. Heartred's "cold and unmoving" (Adams) glare and the Deckers' inevitable bullying before she breaks down. Alice and Allie make it through in the end, but not without some anxiety and confusion afterward.

In the opposite extreme of nonexistence through smallness and invisibility, the unexpected growth spurts that Alice and Allie experience do more metaphorically than make them feel exposed when they would rather be alone. They cause the girls to "[become] defined through a language that [others] have the power to use," while not having "a reciprocal power to define . . the surrounding world" (Turner 248). Alice is unable to make her case of being "a little girl" when the pigeon, furious and terrified at the unexpected appearance of Alice's elongated form, accuses her of being a "serpent" (Carroll 100). In a way no less humiliating, Allie's encounters with the Decker sisters regarding first her torn, outgrown jacket and then her mother's too-large one end up labeling her as a "mouse" and a "freak" (Adams), both constant reminders of Allie's status as an outcast. The same can be said about Charlie: his disability is very different from Allie's, but Mrs. Heartred's condemnation of them both as "beastly"—not unlike the King and Queen's disapproval of Alice growing "a mile high" (Carroll 154) in the court room—attests to how, to some, being insane can be synonymous with being inhuman.

Like many diagnosed with APD, since *Alice* and *Allie*'s characters' "input is frequently off-topic or shows a lack of comprehension of the topic," they are often "ridiculed, laughed at, or—even worse—simply ignored" (Bellis 6). Just as Carroll (or Dodgson) is to this day branded with "an invented biography of an invented name" (Leach 10), Auditory Processing Disorder is still facing some criticism as to its existence and legitimacy as a medical condition. This debate passes on to those for whom the disorder brings constant anguish. Fighting "for the right to say 'I belong'" (Bellis 125) feels like a losing battle as people judge sufferers to the point where the latter can begin to question who they really are, whether they can ever be more than what others believe, or even really learn anything from their experiences.

Notes

1. Charlie's response is based on lines from Hallmark's 1999 T.V. movie adaption of *Alice in Wonderland*:

> White Rabbit: Are you crying?
> Alice: Yes!
> White Rabbit: Well, fortunately, I speak both crying and sobbing fluently!

2. Charlie's question and the abruptness of his inquiries are reminiscent of Alice's encounter with the Caterpillar (Carroll 98). Befuddling remarks aside, so much has happened to Alice by this time that she has become more confused than ever about her own identity.

3. Carroll is said to have suffered from severe stuttering, which was at its worst whenever he was in "unfamiliar or stressful situations" (Woolf 72). Interestingly, he had once stated that "those who did not suffer from 'hesitation', as he called it, could not really imagine what a drawback in life it was" (73).

4.   Lily is based somewhat on Alice's sister from Carroll's story, but even more so upon the sister from Walt Disney's 1951 film version of *Alice in Wonderland*. Like Lily, this latter sister more distinctly expresses frustration at the trouble she has at understanding the unusual mentality of her younger sibling.

5.   Allie's random analogy is a play on the Mad Hatter's famous riddle, "Why is a raven like a writing desk?" Carroll intentionally created this riddle without an answer, but over the years hundreds of people have thought up numerous potential answers for it (Gardner 71-3 n. 5). The fact that Charlie has an answer to Allie's seemingly unsolvable riddle emphasizes the creative abilities of those with speech/auditory impediments which, while capable of being expressed, may often be overlooked or even suppressed.

6.   The March Hare, as originally illustrated by John Tenniel, is shown with bits of straw on his head. In Carroll's time, straw was an artistic symbol of madness (Gardner 66 n. 8).

7.   The bread-and-butterfly is not in Carroll's story, but was created for Disney's

film. It is pointed out to Alice by the talking Red Rose.

8.   One of the many myths surrounding Lewis Carroll is that he suffered from mercury poisoning, though there is little evidence to support this. Mercury was once used in the manufacture of hats. Because of the mental health problems this practice caused, it is thought to have helped spawn the phrase "mad as a hatter" (Gardner 66 n. 8), hence the creation of the Mad Hatter, as well as Charlie's mention of his mother's hat. Today, a common cause of mercury toxicity is the ingesting of contaminated fish and shellfish. Symptoms may include impairment of peripheral vision; disturbances in sensations (a "pins and needles" feeling); lack of movement coordination; impairment of speech, hearing, and walking; and muscle weakness ("Mercury" par 6). Research also suggests that mercury is a factor in cardiovascular disease and can impede "certain heart enzymes necessary for heart muscle contraction" (Trivieri 757-8). Regarding Charlie's claim of "Lady Mercury's messenger," Mercury is also the Roman name of the messenger of the gods.

9.   After Alice tells her older sister about her dreams of Wonderland at the end of Carroll's story, the latter begins imagining

those visions manifesting themselves in real life, and she goes on to reminisce about the pleasures of childlike thinking (Carroll 158-9).

10. In his *Annotated Alice*, Martin Gardner includes a diary entry Carroll once wrote (February 9, 1856) regarding his thoughts on dreaming and insanity (67 n. 9):

> "Query: when we are dreaming and, as often happens, have a dim consciousness of the fact and try to wake, do we not say and do things which in waking life would be insane? May we not then sometimes define insanity as an inability to distinguish which is the waking and which the sleeping life? We often dream without the least suspicion of unreality: 'Sleep hath its own world,' and it is often as lifelike as the other."

11. This is also a reason why *Allie* is written in first-person present tense rather than in third-person omniscient past tense like the original *Alice*. This helps to help better illustrate the limited trains of thought that APD sufferers may tend to retain.

12. One of Carroll's hobbies was amateur photography, though many of his photos, and consequently, he himself, have been described among other things as "voyeuristic" (Kelly 44) because his human subjects were most often young, prepubescent girls.

Author's Note and Works Cited

While *Allie's Adventure on the Wonder* is a work of fiction based on certain plot elements from Lewis Carroll's book *Alice's Adventures in Wonderland*, it should be noted that my claims regarding Auditory Processing Disorder are based solely on my own research and my experiences with it. As of the time this was written, I had not personally met anyone who either suffers from or specializes in the study of APD, and there are various types of the disorder which affect people of both sexes and different ages in a variety of ways depending on how it manifests itself. Thus, my depictions and related arguments are not all-inclusive.

Bellis, Ph.D., Teri James. *When the Brain Can't Hear: Unraveling the Mystery of Auditory Processing Disorder*. New York: Pocket, 2002. Print.

Carroll, Lewis. *Alice's Adventures in Wonderland*. Ed. Richard Kelly. Second ed. Peterborough, Ont.: Broadview, 2011. Print.

Carroll, Lewis and Martin Gardner. ed. *The Annotated Alice: The Definitive*

Edition: *Alice's Adventures in Wonderland & Through the Looking-Glass*. New York: Norton, 2000. Print.

Leach, Karoline. *In the Shadow of the Dreamchild: A New Understanding of Lewis Carroll*. London: Peter Owen, 1999. Print.

"Mercury." *EPA*. Environmental Protection Agency, n.d. Web. 05 Nov. 2012. <http://www.epa.gov/hg/index.html>.

Trivieri, Larry, and John W. Anderson, eds. *Alternative Medicine: The Definitive Guide*. Second ed. Berkeley: Celestial Arts, 2002. Print.

Turner, Beatrice. "'Which Is to Be Master?' Language as Power in *Alice in Wonderland* and *Through the Looking-Glass*." *Children's Literature Association Quarterly* 35.3 (2010): 243-54. *Project MUSE*. The Johns Hopkins University Press, 2012. Web. 01 Nov, 2012. <http://muse.jhu.edu/journals/childrens_literature_association_quarterly/v035/35.3.turner.html>.

Woolf, Jenny. *The Mystery of Lewis Carroll: Discovering the Whimsical, Thoughtful and Sometimes Lonely Man Who Created Alice in Wonderland*. New York, NY: St. Martin's, 2010. Print.

Bios

About the Author

Erika Adams graduated from Lake Superior College with an Associate of Arts degree in 2007 and from UMD with a Bachelor's degree in English in 2013. She was diagnosed with Auditory Processing Disorder before she was two years old and worked with numerous specialists, Special Education advisors, and IEPs to help her both inside and outside of school.

She originally wrote *Allie's Adventure* as part of a creative writing project for a course in Childhood in Literature in Culture in the Fall of 2012. She now hopes that the story will not only entertain fans of the classic *Alice*, but more importantly help raise awareness of APD.

Miss Adams lives in Duluth, Minnesota and is a self-proclaimed book-worm, cross-stitcher, gamer, and anime geek. This is her first book. For more on her writings, check out her Facebook page.

About the Cover Artist

Jordyn Swenson graduated in 2013 with a Bachelor of Fine Arts degree in Graphic Design. Miss Swenson and Miss Adams met each other through the latter's mother.

She is an avid lover of music, horseback-riding, Jeep Wranglers, and junk food. This is her first book cover.